Her Secret Letters

Theva Kiruba

Ukiyoto Publishing

Dedication

The LORD your God will set you high above all the nations on earth. All these blessings will come on you and accompany you if you obey the LORD your God." (Deuteronomy28:1)

Thank you god for your abundant blessings and made this book possible. His name has to be praised in the hallway. He is faithful when I'm faithless. He has done great things in my life. He has raised me from the dust and molded me as an aesthetic colorful Pot.

I extend my sincere gratitude to Dr.Sr. Christina Brigit, Principal of Holy Cross college, Dr. Catherin Edward, Dr.Sr. Judy Gomez, Dr.K.Suganthi, Dr. Cheryl Antonette Dumenil, Ms.Maria Camilla, Mrs.Eileen Brisha and all my English department staff members, Holy Cross college, Trichy, India, for their constant support and motivation

Heartfelt thanks to my parents, Preceleya, Mrs. Devi Shree, Persis Cynthia, friends, all my brothers and sisters, family members for their love and support. My special thanks to my publishing house and the team, who helped to achieve my dream.

Acknowledgement

*"The L*ORD *your God will set you high above all the nations on earth. All these blessings will come on you and accompany you if you obey the L*ORD *your God."* (Deuteronomy28:1)

Thank you god for your abundant blessings and made this book possible. His name has to be praised in the hallway. He is faithful when I'm faithless. He has done great things in my life. He has raised me from the dust and molded me as an aesthetic colorful Pot.

I extend my sincere gratitude to Dr.Sr. Christina Brigit, Principal of Holy Cross college, Dr. Catherin Edward, Dr.Sr. Judy Gomez, Dr.K.Suganthi, Dr. Cheryl Antonette Dumenil, Ms.Maria Camilla, Mrs.Eileen Brisha and all my English department staff members, Holy Cross college, Trichy, India, for their constant support and motivation

Heartfelt thanks to my parents, Preceleya, Mrs. Devi Shree, Persis Cynthia, friends, all my brothers and sisters, family members for their love and support.

My special thanks to my publishing house and the team, who helped to achieve my dream.

Preface

Unlock the secrets of life with this mesmerising collection of poems. From exploring the beauty of nature to the complexities of the human heart, this book is a journey through the joys and sorrows of life.

With vivid imagery and thought-provoking language, this is a book that will stay with you long after you've read it. Each poem will draw you into its world and leave you with a deeper understanding of the beauty and emotion of life.

This book will take you on a journey of self-discovery, reminding you of the power of words and the importance of cherishing the moments that make life so special. Be ready to explore the depths of emotion and find a newfound appreciation for life.

Contents

Life is?

I.

Life is like a journey, winding through time

It can be hard, it can be sublime

We travel through its ups and downs,

Full of mystery, laughter, and frowns

The roads are long, sometimes they're short

And often leave us feeling distraught

But if we look around, we just might find

That life is full of joy, beauty, and surprise

II.

 Life is an adventure, full of twists and turns

And the journey can at times be hard to learn

The highs, the lows, the joys, and the pain

They all make life so much more than mundane

It's a journey of learning, of discovery and growth

And of facing your fears, no matter how much they loathe

Life is an endless ride of uncertainty,

But embracing its beauty is what sets us free

III.

 Life is a roller coaster, full of highs and lows

The drops, the hills, the thrills and woes

Sometimes we feel the joy, and sometimes the despair
But we must keep on going, for there's no one else to care
Life can be beautiful, and it can be cruel
We must navigate our way through its rules
Our destiny is determined by the choices we make
So take the path of courage and never make a mistake

IV.

 Life is a journey, an ever-changing path
Sometimes with joy, at times with wrath
We must learn to take it in stride
No matter how hard we may want to hide
Life is a canvas, so make it your own
Create a masterpiece, never be shown
Life isn't always easy, but it's worth the effort
And soon you'll be rewarded with a life most content

V.

 Life is a game of chance, a spin of the wheel
We must be brave and give it a feel
We never know what will come of us
But if we take risks, we can make a fuss
Life is a challenge, an opportunity to grow
To take the wrong steps, and to make the right ones show
We must strive to make the most of the chances we get
For it's our choices that will ultimately determine our fate

VI.

Life is a book, full of stories untold
It can be opened, or forever left closed
We can be the writer or the reader of the tale
But the best way to live is to jump into the fray
Life is a journey, a page to be filled
With a bit of courage, our future can be sealed
Let us take risks, and never fear the unknown
For courage will bring us closer to our goals

VII.

Life is an ocean, with storms and calm
Sometimes it's filled with joy and sometimes with qualm
It's a ride of waves and troughs, of moments that pass
We must learn to keep our heads above the water's glass
Life is a journey, a tale of adventure and strife
Of courage and strength, of joy and strife
Our courage will be tested, but we must never give up
For life has so much to share, so much to offer us

VIII.

Life is a road, filled with bumps and curves
We must learn to take it in stride and not swerve
It's a path of choices, of dreams that we make
Of possibilities that we can one day partake
Life is a challenge, a gift to be cherished

We must learn to live, and never be perished

We must take our chances, and make the right moves

For life is what we make of it, and it's up to us to choose

IX.

 Life is a battlefield, with battles to fight

Sometimes you win, sometimes you lose your might

It's a fight of courage, of strength and of will

To stand up to challenges, no matter how still

Life is a journey, with dreams to be chased

Of happiness and joy, of victories to be tasted

But it's also a chance to learn and to grow

To make mistakes and to live life in full flow

X.

 Life is a garden, full of beauty and grace

We must learn to nurture it with tenderness and grace

It's a chance to grow and to learn from our mistakes

To make progress and turn the garden into a lake

Life is a journey, a path of trials and tribulations

We must be brave and overcome our inhibitions

We must take risks and never be afraid of the unknown

For life is a journey that can be beautiful and serene

Revelation

Life can be hard and rough,
No matter how much you bluff.
The world can be a demanding place,
Where you'll never find a break.

The future can be a daunting path,
That will always lead to strife.
No matter how much you plan and prepare,
You'll always feel unfulfilled in life.

The journey can be filled with pain,
That never fully goes away.
The struggles so hard to bear,
Where you can't escape your dismay.

The dreams that never come true,
Can make life so hard to cope.
The obstacles so hard to surmount,
Where you can't ever find hope.

The loneliness and emptiness,
That can make life so hard to bear.
It's here where you feel lost,
And can't escape the despair.

The pain that never truly fades,

Is one of life's hardest parts.

The heartache that lingers on,

Where hope just falls apart.

The expectations you can't meet,

Can make it hard to survive.

The pressure that never abates,

Where you can't seem to find a drive.

The disappointments so hard to accept,

That can make life so hard to cope.

The failures so hard to digest,

Where you can't ever seem to find hope.

The moments of despair,

Can be life's hardest struggles.

The moments of sorrow,

Where you just want to hug a bubble.

The feelings of dread,

Can make life so hard to bear.

The moments of fear,

Where you just want to disappear.

The sadness that never ends,

Can make life so hard to cope.

The sorrow that never bends,
Where you can't ever seem to find hope.

The fights that never end,
Can make life so hard to bear.
The arguments that never mend,
Where you just want to get out of there.

The moments of heartbreak,
Can be life's hardest times.
The moments of loneliness,
Where you find it hard to rhyme.

The moments of regret,
Can make life so hard to cope.
The moments of pain,
Where you can't ever seem to find hope.

The moments of sadness,
Where you just want to break down and cry.
The moments of emptiness,
Where you just want to give up and die.

The moments of confusion,
Can be life's hardest part.
The moments of helplessness,
Where you can't ever seem to find hope.

Hunch of Bunch

A deep emotion so strong, a feeling that lingers on.

It's hard to explain, but it's not something that's gone.

It's a feeling I'm sure you know, that you can't fully describe.

It's a powerful emotion that's felt deep inside.

It's a feeling that brings joy, but can cause pain.

It's a feeling that can last, and remain the same.

It can bring a tear to your eye, with a sorrowful cry.

It's a feeling that won't just pass you by.

It's a feeling that can be felt, that can't be seen.

It's a feeling that can bring happiness, or make you scream.

It's a feeling that takes hold, and refuses to let go.

It's a feeling that can really make you grow.

It can be a feeling of love, and a feeling of fear.

It can be a feeling of joy, when life is unclear.

It can be a feeling of sorrow, when life isn't fair.

It's a feeling that can make you aware.

It's a feeling that can make you strong, or break you down.

It's a feeling that can turn your heart around.

It's a feeling that can make you smile, or make you frown.

It's a feeling that will stay with you, long after it's gone.

Branch of Solitude

Lonely life, a life of pain,
A life of sadness, without gain,
Stillness fills the air, so still,
My heart, a well of ill will.

My days are filled with tears and sorrow,
My life a path of no tomorrow,
No one knows my inner strife,
No one hears my silent cry.

My thoughts, a constant haze,
My feelings, always a maze,
Fear and loneliness, my daily friend,
A life without a happy end.

But hope is there, deep down inside,
A longing for a better life to come,
But until that day, I'll stay alone,
Lonely life, a life of my own.

Fruit of Reward

Happy life is a sweet reward,

A blessing that can't be ignored.

It's the moments that make us smile,

Where the love of those around us is worthwhile.

It's the little things that matter,

The everyday joys that can scatter.

From the laughter of a child,

To a hug that warms us for a while.

Happy life is a beautiful thing,

It's something that can make our heart sing.

From the joy of a summer day,

To the sky that's filled with stars and the moon's ray.

Happy life is a journey of delight,

A path that's filled with light.

It's embracing the beauty and grace,

And cherishing all the moments that take place.

Misery Bag

A sorrowful life, so hard to bear,

No joy, no love, no pleasure there,

No friends, no family, just me alone,

Lingering in a desolate home,

The days seem endless, the nights so blue,

My dreams of happiness shattered and through,

No hope for a brighter tomorrow,

Just sadness and loneliness to follow,

A sorrowful life with no end in sight,

No joy, no laughter, no respite in light,

My heart and soul are heavy and sad,

And life feels so utterly mad,

No way out of this wretched despair,

No sign of sunshine anywhere,

No one to show me the way,

My sorrowful life I'm forced to stay.

Two souls and one heart!

You and I together, like birds in flight

We soar and glide, so graceful and light

Our love is so beautiful, it fills me with glee

It's a feeling that I can never see

Each moment we share, is like a dream

Our two hearts become one, it's all so serene

We can feel the passion, coming from deep within

And know that our love will never end

Our bond is so strong, like nothing else

It can never be broken, no matter the test

Through our highs and lows, we never give up

Our commitment, our love, is all that we need to keep

Our love is understanding, our hearts beat as one

We are by each other's side, even when the night is done

And in the morning, when we wake

We look into each other's eyes, and all that we can take

Our love is a blessing, so strong and so true

It makes us so happy, to love one another like we do

We'll forever cherish, these moments of love

That we share together, up high above

Our love is divine, like a miracle in motion
It fills us with joy and emotion
Breaking the barriers, of time and space
And reminding us of what we can embrace

Our love is a journey, unfolding as we go
Our two hearts one, forever aglow
We are so connected, so deeply intertwined
Our love will never die, it will always be alive

Despair in nowhere!

I.

A deep heart wound that lingers on,

I can't seem to shake it off.

A pain so deep, it goes so far,

It dwells in my heart like a scar.

It's a wound that never leaves,

No matter how hard I try to grieve.

It's a pain that's here to stay,

No matter what I do or say.

The pain just won't go away,

It follows me night and day.

No matter how hard I try to hide,

It remains in my heart so wide.

It's a deep and aching pain,

It can never be contained.

It's a wound that will never heal,

It will only continue to steal.

My memories, my joy, and my peace,

It takes it away, never to cease.

A deep heart wound that lingers on,

This sorrow will forever be gone.

II.

A deep heart wound that burns inside,

It's there no matter how hard I try.

A pain so deep, it won't go away,

It lingers in my heart all day.

It's a wound that will never fade,

No matter what I do or say.

It's a pain that lingers on,

No matter how hard I try to move on.

The pain just won't go away,

It follows me night and day.

No matter how hard I try to forget,

It remains in my heart so deep.

It's a deep and aching pain,

It can never be contained.

It's a wound that will never heal,

It will only continue to steal.

My happiness, my love, and my dreams,

It takes it away, never to cease.

A deep heart wound that lingers on,

This sorrow will forever be gone.

III.

A deep heart wound that never fades,

It's a pain that's here to stay.

A hurt so deep, it won't go away,

It lingers in my heart all day.

It's a wound that never goes away,

No matter how hard I try to stay.

It's a pain that's here to stay,

No matter what I do or say.

The pain just won't go away,

It follows me night and day.

No matter how hard I try to erase,

It remains in my heart in this place.

It's a deep and aching pain,

It can never be contained.

It's a wound that will never heal,

It will only continue to steal.

My love, my joy, and my peace,

It takes it away, never to cease.

A deep heart wound that lingers on,

This sorrow will forever be gone.

IV.

A deep heart wound that I can't fix,
It's a pain that lingers on and on.
A hurt so deep, it won't go away,
It lingers in my heart all day.

It's a wound that never fades,
No matter how hard I try to stay.
It's a pain that's here to stay,
No matter what I do or say.

The pain just won't go away,
It follows me night and day.
No matter how hard I try to ignore,
It remains in my heart evermore.

It's a deep and aching pain,
It can never be contained.
It's a wound that will never heal,
It will only continue to steal.

My hope, my dreams, and my love,
It takes it away, never to cease.
A deep heart wound that lingers on,
This sorrow will forever be gone.

V.

A deep heart wound that never heals,

It's a pain that lingers on and on.

A hurt so deep, it won't go away,

It lingers in my heart all day.

It's a wound that never fades,

No matter how hard I try to stay.

It's a pain that's here to stay,

No matter what I do or say.

The pain just won't go away,

It follows me night and day.

No matter how hard I try to deny,

It remains in my heart forever.

Anxious Butterflies

I.
Fear of life within my core,
My mind reels, my heart it soars,
I spin in circles, my thoughts unknown,
My worries linger, like a stone.

I feel my breath begin to seize,
My heart races, my skin a freeze,
My mind's a mess, my sanity a blur,
My fear of life has taken over.

II.
 My fear of life has taken hold,
I can't seem to break the mold,
My thoughts scattered, my dreams unknown,
My fears linger, like a tone.

My future feels so far away,
My strength and courage left astray,
My will is weak, my courage is a blur,
My fear of life has taken over.

III. Fear of life has taken me,
I can't seem to set myself free,

My worries linger, like a song,

My courage fades, I feel so wrong.

My life feels so out of control,

My soul aches for a goal,

My mind's a mess, my sanity a blur,

My fear of life has taken over.

IV. Fear of life has taken me,

I can't seem to break the spell,

My thoughts rush, my heart it beats,

My courage is lost, my future bleak.

My strength has failed me, it's gone,

My will is weak, I can't go on,

My mind's a mess, my sanity a blur,

My fear of life has taken over.

V. Fear of life has me in fear,

My courage lost and far from near,

My thoughts a haze, my soul a blur,

My courage is fading, my will is unsure.

My life a mystery, my dreams destroyed,

My heart is heavy, my courage all but void,

My mind's a mess, my sanity a blur,

My fear of life has taken over.

VI. Fear of life has taken me,
My courage lacking, my will so weak,
My mind's a blur, my heart it beats,
My courage lost, my future bleak.

My life has changed, I can't go back,
My hopes and dreams now all but lack,
My mind's a mess, my sanity a blur,
My fear of life has taken over.

VII. Fear of life has taken me,
My courage lost, my will so weak,
My thoughts a haze, my soul a blur,
My courage is fading, my future is dark.

My strength and courage weak and gone,
My will is lost, I can't go on,
My mind's a mess, my sanity a blur,
My fear of life has taken over.

VIII. Fear of life has taken my heart,
My courage lost, my will apart,
My thoughts a mess, my soul a blur,
My courage is fading, my future is dark.

Where once I found strength and hope,
I'm now so lost, I can't cope,

My mind's a mess, my sanity a blur,
My fear of life has taken over.

IX. Fear of life has taken me,
My courage lost, my will so weak,
My thoughts a mess, my soul a blur,
My courage is fading, my future bleak.

My heart is heavy, my spirit so low,
My dreams are gone, I can't go on,
My mind's a mess, my sanity a blur,
My fear of life has taken over.

X. Fear of life has taken me,
My courage failing, my will so weak,
My thoughts a mess, my soul a blur,
My courage is fading, my future is dark.

My strength and courage now all but gone,
My will is lost, my heart so wrong,
My mind's a mess, my sanity a blur,
My fear of life has taken over.

Hammer under the blanket

Life can be worse in many ways,

It can bring us to our knees,

It can make us miserable,

It can cause us to freeze.

It can take away our joy,

It can make us feel so low,

It can take away our laughter,

And send us into a woe.

It can make us feel helpless,

It can take away our pride,

It can make us feel worthless,

And make us run and hide.

It can bring us despair,

It can make our dreams evaporate,

It can rob us of our hope,

And make our future seem so great.

It can make us question our purpose,

It can make us feel so small,

It can make us feel like we don't belong,

And make us feel so alone.

It can take away our dreams,
And make us want to give up,
It can make us feel like nothing matters,
And make us feel like a pup.

It can make us feel like failures,
And make us feel like we can't cope,
It can make us feel like our lives are pointless,
And make us feel like we don't have hope.

It can take away our courage,
And make us feel so scared,
It can make us feel like we're worthless,
And make us feel so unprepared.

It can make us feel like no one cares,
It can make us feel so lost,
It can make us feel so helpless,
And make us pay the cost.

It can make us so depressed,
And make us feel so dejected,
It can make us feel like life is meaningless,
And make us feel so disconnected.

It can make us feel so alone,
It can make us feel so empty,
It can make us feel like we're in a dark hole,
And make us feel so heavy.

It can take away our joy,
And make us feel so sad,
It can make us feel like we're in a dark abyss,
And make us feel so bad.

It can make us feel like we're drowning,
It can make us feel so low,
It can make us feel like our dreams have vanished,
And leave us with nowhere to go.

It can make us feel like we're not worthy,
It can make us feel so small,
It can make us feel like life is pointless,
And make us feel like we've hit a wall.

It can take away our light,
It can make us feel so scared,
It can make us feel like we can't escape,
And make us feel so unprepared.

It can make us feel like we're stuck,
It can make us feel so helpless,

It can make us feel like we're on our own,
And make us feel so worthless.

It can make us feel so broken,
Like we can't get back up,
It can make us feel like we're in a prison,
And make us feel so stuck.

It can make us feel like life is over,
It can make us feel so low,
It can make us feel like our dreams will never come true,
And make us feel so slow.

It can make us forget our goals,
It can make us feel so empty,
It can make us feel like there's no point in living,
And make us feel so heavy.

It can make us feel so hopeless,
And make us feel so lost,
It can make us feel like we have nothing to look forward to,
And make us feel so frost.

It can make us feel so isolated,
It can make us feel so alone,
It can make us feel like we're in a dark abyss,
And make us feel like we're not shown.

It can take away our motivation,
And make us feel so drained,
It can make us feel like we're in a jail cell,
And make us feel so chained.
It can make us feel so dark,
It can make us feel so depressed,
It can make us feel like life is meaningless,
And make us feel so oppressed.

It can make us feel so small,
It can make us feel so lost,
It can make us feel like our dreams are impossible,
And make us feel like the cost.

It can make us feel so helpless,
It can make us feel so scared,
It can make us feel like we have no control,
And make us feel so impaired.

Twinge my Heart

I.

My heart is so heavy and I feel so alone,

Lost in the darkness and feeling so low,

My days are so long and the nights so cold,

I can't bear the pain, it's unbearable, I'm told.

My friends have moved on and I'm left behind,

My life is a cold, dark, lonely kind,

I'm so very tired, I can't stand the strain,

But I can't bear the thought of never seeing her again.

I search for the one that my heart yearns for,

But all I find is an empty, aching door,

The pain in my chest is almost too much to bear,

My heart broken, I'm drowning in despair.

II

The pain of her absence is piercing my soul,

My tears wash away my aching and sorrow,

I'm desperate to find the one I love so,

But I'm trapped here in this lonely world below.

My heart is so heavy and I feel so low,

The pain of her absence never lets me go,

I'm desperate to feel her embrace once more,

But my dreams just bring me pain galore.

My days are so long and my nights so cold,

I fear I'll never feel her warmth ever again,

My heart is aching, my tears never cease,

I'm so lonely, I can't bear this pain, I'm at peace.

III

My heart is so heavy and I feel so alone,

Lost in this desolation, so far from home,

My days are so long and the nights so cold,

I just wish I could be with her, to never be alone.

I'm so very tired, I can't stand the strain,

I'm desperate to find the one that I love so,

To feel her embrace and to be in her company,

But I'm trapped in this lonely world, so far away.

The pain of her absence is too much to bear,

My heart broken, I just want to be there,

My heart aches and my tears never cease,

Lonely and broken, I can't bare this pain, I'm at peace.

Betwixt Nowhere!

Trapped between four walls of tears,

I feel so utterly alone,

Living in this world of fears,

No matter where I roam.

My heart is heavy with despair,

My spirit broken and lost,

My soul is filled with loneliness,

No matter how much it costs.

The four walls close in around me,

Darkness closing in from all sides,

My heart is filled with misery,

My strength and will, nowhere to hide.

My soul is lost in a void,

My energy completely drained,

My life spent in a void,

Living within these four walls, I'm lost and pained.

Voiceless Echoes

I.
Sitting between these four walls,
I feel so small and so alone
My heart is so heavy,
Crying out in a mournful tone.

My body feels so heavy,
And my spirit has been drained,
My energy is completely sapped,
My heart and soul remain pained.

The loneliness is overwhelming,
My mind is filled with despair,
I cannot escape this prison,
This life of darkness and despair.

II
My soul is in a prison
Trapped between four walls
My heart is so heavy,
Loneliness comes and appalls.

My energy is all but gone,
My spirit nearly drained,

My heart is filled with sadness,
Pain and sorrow remains.
I've been living in darkness,
The walls don't let me breathe,
This loneliness swallows me,
My soul is in deep grief.

III

I'm living between these four walls
My spirit is lost and drained
My energy is sapped away
My heart and soul remain pained.

My loneliness is overwhelming,
I'm lost and filled with despair
The walls won't let me go,
The darkness is everywhere.

My soul is stuck in prison,
It's so hard to break free,
I'm all alone and scared,
Filled with misery.

In the Parrot's cell

I am stuck in this caged life,

The walls close around me in strife,

I feel so confined, my heart can not take,

I yearn for freedom, for my soul to awake.

Living in this caged life,

I have been here for far too long,

My wings yearn to be set free,

So I can fly high, and be truly me.

My life here is but a jail,

I can no longer bear this tale,

I want to break free, soar through the sky,

Leave this life of cage, let loose my cry.

This caged life has taken it's toll,

I must break free and leave this hole,

My wings will stretch and I will fly,

Live my life and bid goodbye.

My shackles will be broken,

And my spirit will be awoken,

For I will rise and fly away,

In the sky I will stay.

My dreams of freedom I will seek,
For forever I have been so meek,
The sky will be my play ground,
The sun will be my crown.

My caged life was my prison,
But now I am living my mission,
To fly above the clouds,
To make my dreams come out loud.

My heart will never be still,
For I have tasted freedom's thrill,
My wings will soar and I will be,
Living life with only glee.

My life in the cage is done,
No more will I be so glum,
My horizons will stretch ever so wide,
My spirit will fly and I will abide.

Torn Flesh

My heart's been wounded deep,
So deep that it scarcely bleeds.
It's been broken so many times,
I'm sure I'm gonna break.

My soul has been battered and bruised,
And I'm left with these wounds.
I'm left with this pain that won't go away,
It's here to stay.

I've been hurt so much,
I can't even imagine.
My heart has been broken and my soul's been crushed,
And now I'm just numb.

Too many times I've been let down,
Fooled by those I once trusted.
My heart has been broken and my soul's been bruised,
But I must keep on going.

II.
My heart has been wounded and torn,
By those who I once loved.

I'm left with these scars that never heal,
No matter how hard I try.
My soul has been battered and bruised,
Through all the pain I've endured.
And I'm left here with these wounds,
That will never truly heal.

I've been hurt so many times,
I can't even begin to count.
My heart has been broken and my soul's been crushed,
And I can't even look in the mirror.

Too many times I've been let down,
By those who said they'd never leave.
My heart has been broken and my soul's been bruised,
But I must keep on going.

III.
My heart has been wounded and torn,
By those who I thought were friends.
I'm left with these scars that never heal,
No matter how hard I cry.

My soul has been battered and bruised,
Through all the pain I've faced.
And I'm left here with these wounds,
That will never truly fade.

I've been hurt so many times,
That I don't even know who I am.
My heart has been broken and my soul's been crushed,
And I can barely even breathe.

Too many times I've been let down,
By those who said they'd never hurt me.
My heart has been broken and my soul's been bruised,
But I must keep on going.

Pine's Thirst

I yearn for a life of freedom,
From the hell I find myself in,
A life of joy and pleasure,
Where I can be a part of heaven.

A life of peace and harmony,
Away from all the strife and pain,
Where I can be free to be me,
And gain the power to live again.

A life of love and understanding,
Where I'm surrounded by the sun,
Where I can explore the world around me,
And be thankful when it's done.

A life of hope and optimism,
Where I don't have to worry or fear,
Where I can feel the warmth of love,
And happiness that's always near.

A life of beauty and grace,
Where I can be content and free,
Where I can live with no regrets,
In heavenly life on earth, I plea.

Broken Wings!

I

.The broken wing that drags me down,

A burden too heavy to bear,

From trauma in society, I can't move on,

My kitchen sink my only haven, No room to breathe.

The war inside me never ends,

My path is blocked by heartache,

Crippled by the pain of society,

My kitchen sink my only haven, No room to breathe.

II.

My broken wing a symbol of despair,

A heavy weight of suffering,

Trauma in society has taken its toll,

My kitchen sink my only haven, No room to breathe.

The tears that fall I cannot stop,

My heart an open wound so sore,

The never ending war within me rages on,

My kitchen sink my only haven, No room to breathe.

III.

My broken wing a metaphor for life,

Trauma in society has taken its toll,

My heart not ready to surrender,

My kitchen sink my only haven, No room to breathe.

The war within me has no end,

My path blocked by sorrows and pain,

A battle I cannot win on my own,

My kitchen sink my only haven, No room to breathe.

IV.

The broken wing that drags me down,

A war inside so I cannot sleep,

Living in the pain of society,

My kitchen sink my only haven, No room to breathe.

My heart an open wound of hurt,

My dreams blocked by constant pain,

A never ending war within me rages on,

My kitchen sink my only haven, No room to breathe.

V.

My broken wing a constant reminder,

A heavy weight of sorrow and pain,

Trauma in society has taken its toll,

My kitchen sink my only haven, No room to breathe.

The tears that fall, I cannot stop,

My heart an open wound with no cure,

The never ending war within me rages on,

My kitchen sink my only haven, No room to breathe.

Her Strain

I.

She lingers in a room of shadows and strife,

Her spirit broken, her thoughts filled with strife.

The walls seem to whisper with hollow strains,

Her heart heavy, her future unclear and unfound.

This girl, she has seen more than her share of pain,

That has left her feeling helpless and bound.

But despite it all, she perseveres and holds on tight,

To the hope that one day she'll find the light.

II.

She's been through so much, yet still she stands tall,

Her spirit undeterred, she'll not take a fall.

She looks for the good, despite the bad that clouds her way,

Knowing that one day her struggles will pay.

She looks for the future, the windows that open,

And she'll never forget that the light is out there hopin'.

III.

This girl, her will is strong, she won't give in,

She'll fight till the end, to see the light again.

Tears in her eyes, and a broken heart,

But she won't give in, she'll make a new start.

Through her pain, she'll keep searching for the sun,

A new life awaits her, her struggles will be done.

IV.

She stands in the dark, with a heart so full of strife,

Her future so uncertain, her courage put to the test.

She knows the light is out there, and it's only a matter of time,

Until she finds it, her spirit will remain sublime.

She'll fight every day, and look for that glimmer of hope,

That will guide her steps, and bring her out of this dark place she's in.

V.

She stands in the dark, and looks for the light,

Her courage and spirit, it never fades from sight.

She'll never give up, no matter how hard it may seem,

She knows the sun will come, and bring her out of her dream.

She's been through so much, but her courage remains true,

And one day soon, the light will shine through.

Hazy Night

I.

A girl's dream, a distant shore

The journey long, the struggle more

Each step she takes, each breath she breathes

A hundred years of battle she believes

The fire within, the drive to succeed

Her heart and soul, a worthy creed

Onward she goes, no time to pause

Through mountains high and valleys low, she soars

II.

Though life may try to keep her down

Her spirit will not be found bound

To the pain and fear, she'll hold no debt

Her dream will rise above the threat

From broken dreams, she'll rise anew

From dark depths, her light will shine through

And when she reaches her destination

The world will see her determination

III.

For each obstacle, each trial and test

She'll strive forward, she won't rest

Her faith will guide her through the night

Every step she'll take with all her might
And when the battle has been fought
Her dream will shine, a glimmering thought
What started as a distant shore
Will be made real, forevermore

IV.

Though the path may twist and turn
Her dreams she'll earn, her courage burn
A hundred years of war, her will she'll prove
No matter what, she'll never lose
From each hardship she'll rise again,
A warrior she'll remain
Her courage strong, her heart of gold
Her dreams will be made, a story told

V.

For every struggle, every fear
This girl will remain true and clear
No obstacles will keep her from her goal
No matter the cost, she'll fill her role
A hundred years of battle to make her dreams come true
This is her story, and she will pursue
One day her dream will be accomplished
And her story will remain, never to be vanquished

Her Resilience

I.

A girl can achieve anything if she desires,
Her hard work and dedication serves her no liars.
Her ambition and dreams she can make come true,
For she knows she deserves it and can make it through.

Her strength and courage will drive her forever,
And she will achieve anything she endeavors.
No matter the challenge, no matter the cost,
Her goals and aspirations she will not loss.

She will honor her dreams and never give in,
For she believes in herself and knows she can win.
She will strive to succeed and push the boundaries,
And the obstacles that come her way she will surmount.

For she is strong and independent,
Achieving her goals is confidently evident.
No matter the hindrance that may stand in her path,
She will do what she sets out to do, she will do the math.

Her hard work will pay off as her dreams come to life,
And she will reach the top and thrive.
For she can do anything and achieve her goals,

For she knows she deserves it, and she has what it takes to go.

II.

A girl can achieve whatever she desires,

For her hard work she surely deserves.

No matter what she sets out to do,

She can make the impossible possible too.

She will go after her dreams without fear,

And she knows her hard work will be her gear.

She will take on the toughest of tasks,

And she will do her best to never ask.

She will make her dreams come alive,

With the strength of her will she will survive.

No matter the obstacles she may face,

She will stand tall and never lose her grace.

She will strive for success and never lose her hope,

For her heart is strong and her will is full of scope.

Her determination will carry her far,

And she will make her dreams her own little star.

No matter how tough the journey may be,

She will never give up and she will succeed.

A girl can achieve anything she sets her mind to,

For she knows she deserves it and she will break through.

III.

A girl can achieve anything she desires,

For her hard work her dreams surely conspire.

She will stand firm in the face of adversity,

For she knows she deserves it and is full of tenacity.

She will strive to reach her goals and make her dreams come true,

No matter how hard the journey may be she will push through.

She will never give up no matter the cost,

For she is determined and the obstacles she will toss.

She will be brave and never lose her strength,

For she knows she deserves it and can go the length.

She will take on the toughest of tasks,

For her strong will and courage will do the math.

She will reach for the highest of heights,

Make her dreams come alive with all her might.

No matter the hardships she may face,

She will never give up and reach her own space.

For she can do anything and achieve any goal,

For she knows she deserves it and has the power to go.

A girl can achieve whatever she wants to,

For her hard work she deserves it, that is true.

IV.

A girl can achieve anything she desires,

For her hard work she certainly deserves.

She will strive to reach her goals and make her dreams come true,

For she knows she can make it and will push through.

No matter the obstacles and the challenge she may face,

She will never lose her strength and grace.

Her ambition and dedication will lead her to success,

For she is brave and determined and will never digress.

She will never give up no matter what comes her way,

For her dreams she will strive and never shy away.

She will take on the toughest of tasks,

And she will do her best to never ask.

Her hard work and dedication will pay off in the end,

And she will reach the top and make her dreams her own best friend.

No matter the hardships she may face,

She will never give up and find her own place.

For she can do anything and achieve any goal,

For she knows she deserves it and has the power and control.

A girl can achieve whatever she wants to,

For her hard work she deserves it, and she will get through.

V.

A girl can achieve whatever she desires,

For her hard work her dreams will never tire.

No matter the challenge and the obstacles she face in her life!

Sole Drive!

I.

Girl need no one, that's what she'll say
After every set back and pain she'll stay
She's strong, she knows the way
Her confidence will never be swayed
From her heart she'll never run away

She'll come stronger every single day
Nothing will keep her from her own way
No matter what comes her way
She'll keep on pushing further and further away

She'll never be taken down by anyone's say
She'll never let another make her feel dismay
Girl need no one, that's her truth
She'll come out bigger and better than before, that's her proof

II.

Girl need no one, that's what she'll prove
After every set back and pain she'll move
She'll carry on with her heart held high
No matter what she'll never say die

Her soul is untouchable, her strength unstoppable

She'll carry on with her own flow

She'll never be brought down low

For her, it's always onward and up she'll go

No matter the pain or the struggle she'll face

Her spirit will always remain the same

Girl need no one, she'll make it clear

She'll always come out even stronger than before, that's her fear

III.

Girl need no one, she'll make them believe

After every set back and pain she'll still achieve

She'll never be held back by the weight of the world

She'll take the hits and keep moving forward

Her heart will keep her going, her soul will keep her strong

She'll never be brought down by the negative throng

She'll keep on pushing and keep on striving

No matter what comes she'll keep on surviving

She'll never let a setback bring her down

She'll never let another make her frown

Girl need no one, that's her pride

She'll come out stronger than before, she won't hide

IV.

Girl need no one, that she'll make clear

After every set back and pain she'll stay near

She'll never let anyone take away her will

She'll fight for the life she wants to fill

She'll keep going no matter what comes her way

She'll never let anyone stand in her way

Her spirit will never be broken

She'll keep moving forward and never stay open

She'll never be taken down by anyone's creed

She'll never let another make her bleed

Girl need no one, that she will show

She'll come out stronger than before, that's her goal

V.

Girl need no one, that's her stand

After every set back and pain she'll still land

She'll never be taken down by another's hand

She'll keep on pushing and fight for what she can

Her determination will never be broken

She'll take the hits and keep on going

She'll never let herself get taken down

She'll pick herself up and keep spinning around

She'll never be brought down by anyone's scorn

She'll never let another make her forlorn

Girl need no one, that's her strength

She'll come out stronger than before, however long the length.

Pursuit of Self

I.

I won't wait for someone to tell me I'm great,

I know it, and I'm not afraid to say.

My worth is not defined by anyone else's fate,

I must learn to love and accept myself today.

My courage will grow with each passing day,

No longer letting fear stand in my way.

II.

I will not be ashamed of mistakes I make,

A lesson learned is worth the pain.

I'll use them to help me grow, not break,

Loving myself means I accept the gains.

My inner strength will never be feign,

It will carry me through rain and shine.

III.

I will embrace every part of me,

The good, the bad, and even the ugly.

I may never be everyone's cup of tea,

But that's okay, I need not comply.

My worth is not measured by money or popularity,

I will learn to love myself unconditionally.

IV.

I will look at myself in the mirror and smile,

No longer letting my flaws define me.

I will be patient, kind and compassionate,

My self love will set me free.

I will make sure that my needs are met,

And stop seeking approval from others to be happy.

V.

I will be mindful of the words I say,

I will speak kindly to myself.

I will practice self-care everyday,

Taking time to nurture my mental health.

I will stop comparing myself to others and their way,

My journey is my own and I'll live it my way.

VI.

I will make my dreams come true,

I will not let anyone hold me back.

I will make sure that I am heard,

My worth is not up for attack.

I will focus on what I can do,

Being proud of myself for all that I pursue.

Never Ending Journey!

I.
Love is never ending and it comes from within,
Seek it out and you'll know that you can begin,
To fill your heart with warmth and joy to share,
Self-love is the key to unlocking care.

II.
 To love yourself is to never fear,
Give yourself room to breathe and be sincere,
This love is the most stable of all,
And will be the foundation you stand tall.

III. Believe in yourself, for this is true love,
It's an essence that comes from up above,
Letting go of doubts and worries too,
Find inner peace and love that's true.

IV. Self-love is more than just a phrase,
It's a feeling that will always stay,
Trust yourself and hold onto this truth,
And you'll find never ending love for you.

V. Loving yourself can let you grow,
You'll find happiness that you can show,

Inner strength will come to be,

When you embrace self love eternally.

VI. Take a moment and just be still,

Allow yourself to take the hill,

Your love is something that will never end,

Just look within and find your friend.

VII. Open up your heart and let love in,

A never ending love from deep within,

Accept yourself and who you are,

Your self-love will take you far.

VIII. The love for yourself is so divine,

Expressing it will give you shine,

It's the kind of love that never fades,

And will always be in your heart's shades.

IX. You are unique and you are special,

Your love for yourself will be essential,

Open your heart and let it overflow,

To never ending love you can bestow.

X. Self-love is the most powerful emotion,

Ignite it and you'll find devotion,

Embrace your power and be strong,

For never ending love will last long.

Soul Mechanic

I.

My mind's so often molded by a world that's so unkind,

A place where people put me down and act so unrefined.

Though I try to stay strong, I find those hurtful words linger,

My feelings so often twisted by an insidious wringer.

II.

 Each day I'm molded by the negative that I hear,

The voices in my head won't let me feel any cheer.

My feelings are so often manipulated and so unkempt,

The words I allow in shape my life and I am left soempt.

III.

I strive to keep my heart safe from the hate and the slander,

But still it eats away at me and makes me feel like a cancer.

My mind's so often filled with those negative lies,

Making me feel so discouraged and filled with such demise.

IV.

 I'm trying to shape my thoughts and feelings with positivity,

But it's so hard to do when all I see is animosity.

My mind and heart are molded by all that I have seen,

But I'm fighting to make sure I break free from this mean.

V.

 I'm molding my mind to be the best I can be,

Letting go of the hatred and the negativity.

I'm chiseling away at the walls I have built,

Searching for the peace and joy that I thought I had quelled.

VI.

 I'm striving to stay positive and view things differently,

To rise above the darkness and find a way to be free.

My feelings and thoughts are being molded, I can tell,

I'm slowly learning to love myself and how to break this spell.

VII. I'm doing my best to not be influenced by what I'm told,

To be my own person and remain strong and bold.

My feelings and mind are being molded by those around me,

But I'm determined to stay true to me despite society's plea.

VIII.

 I'm so often molded by those who hurt me and try to bring me
down,

But I'm slowly learning to stand up and wear my own crown.

My thoughts and feelings are in the process of becoming my own,

And I know I will soon find peace and I will be shown.

IX.

 I'm starting to shape my mind and feelings and make them mine,

Ignoring the outside noise and the pressure of the hard times.

My feelings and mind are being molded by the struggles I've faced,

But I'm determined to find the strength to make it through this place.

X.

 I'm on a journey to mold my mind and feelings to be me,

To fill it with my own thoughts and emotions that are free.

My feelings and mind will be molded by my own will and strength,

And I will find the courage to break away from this length.

Daring Dream

I.

I've never been one to back down,
To shy away and hide my frown;
My dreams, they are too important,
So I will always fight for them, no matter what.

My courage and strength within,
Will always help me to begin;
My will and determination,
Will never waiver, no hesitation.

I'll take a stand and be bold,
I'll never give up, never grow cold;
I'm fighting for something that's mine,
My courage will never be denied.

No matter what comes my way,
My strength will never fade away;
My ambition and boldness,
Will keep me on the path, I will confess.

My journey is hard but worthwhile,
My determination and passion, so bright;
I will keep on fighting,

My dreams are worth the effort and striving.

II.

My dreams are something special,

My courage and strength are essential;

I will never stop pushing,

For something I'm passionately pushing.

No matter the obstacles I face,

I will never give in, no disgrace;

My courage and strength within,

Will be my guide and help me begin.

My determination and ambition,

Will take me to the next position;

I'm fighting for what I believe in,

My will will never waiver and thin.

My courage and will never be denied,

My dreams are worth the fight, I can't hide;

My ambition and boldness,

Will keep me on the right path, I profess.

I'm fighting for something that's mine,

My courage and strength will never decline;

My dreams are worth the effort and striving,

My ambition will never stop driving.

III.

My dreams are something special,

My ambition and courage, so essential;

No matter the obstacles I face,

I will never give in, no disgrace.

My determination and passion, so bright,

Will take me to the next height;

I'm fighting for what I believe in,

My courage and strength will never thin.

My ambition and boldness,

Will keep me on the right path, I confess;

I'm fighting for something that's mine,

My will will never waiver and decline.

My courage will never be denied,

My dreams are worth the fight, I can't hide;

My journey is hard but worthwhile,

My determination and passion, so bright.

I will keep on fighting,

My dreams are worth the effort and striving;

My strength will never fade away,

My ambition will never stop driving.

IV.

I've never been one to back down,

My dreams, they are too important;

My will and determination,

Will never waiver, no hesitation.

My courage and strength within,

Will help me to begin;

I'll take a stand and be bold,

I'll never give up, never grow cold.

My ambition and boldness,

Will keep me on the path, I will confess;

I'm fighting for something that's mine,

My courage will never be denied.

My determination and passion, so bright,

Will take me to the next height;

My courage and strength will never decline,

My dreams are worth the fight, I can't hide.

My journey is hard but worthwhile,

My ambition will never stop driving;

My strength will never fade away,

My dreams are worth the effort and striving.

V.

My courage and will never be denied,

My courage and strength are essential;

My ambition and boldness,

Will keep me on the path, I will profess.

I'm fighting for something that's mine,

My determination and passion, so bright;

My will will never waiver and thin,

No matter the obstacles I face, I will never give in.

My dreams are something special,

My courage and strength will never decline;

My ambition will never stop driving,

My journey is hard but worthwhile.

I've never been one to back down,

My dreams, they are too important;

My courage and strength within,

Will always help me to begin.

My determination and ambition,

Will take me to the next position;

I will keep on fighting,

My dreams are worth the effort and striving.

Ceaseless War

I.

Life is a non-stop race, I must keep up my pace

Time is of the essence, I mustn't lag behind

Every day is a challenge, I must stay ahead

I gotta hustle hard and keep my focus instead

II.

 Life is a never-ending race, I must push the limits of my strength

I must find the courage to keep running, despite feeling spent

I must stay in the lead, no matter how hard the course

Though it's filled with uphill climbs, I must keep my poise

III.

 Life is a journey full of tests, I must be ready to persevere

My will is put to the test, I must stay inspired

I must stay focused and believe in myself, no matter how tough

To reach the finish line and realize my dreams, I mustn't give up

IV.

 Life is a continuous race, I must find the courage to go on

The obstacles in my path, I must learn to overcome

I must keep pushing forward and never surrender, no matter what

The finish line is my goal, and I must stay strong

V.

 Life is an ever-changing race, I must stay prepared for its unknowns
In the face of adversity, I must stand my ground
No matter how hard it gets, I must keep my faith alive
My dreams are my guiding light, and I mustn't let them die

VI.

 Life is a never-ending race, I must keep striving to make my mark
I must take on each challenge, no matter how hard the task
No matter how long the journey, I mustn't ever lose sight
My strength is within me, and I must use it to stay in the fight

VII.

 Life is a non-stop race, I must work hard to reach my dreams
I must rise up to each challenge and never give in to fear
Though the odds may be against me, I must never fail to try
My dreams are my strength, and I must keep them alive

VIII.

 Life is an ongoing race, I must focus on my goals
I must stay determined and never give up, no matter how hard the
road
My faith is stronger than ever, and I mustn't let it go
I must take each step with courage, and I must never let it show

IX.

 Life is a ceaseless race, I must keep pushing myself to go beyond

I must find the courage to keep running, even when I'm tired and worn

I must stay ahead of the pack and never give in to fear

My dreams are my compass, and I must find the strength to steer

X.

 Life is a never-ending race, I must stay focused on my dreams

I must take on each challenge, no matter how tough it seems

I mustn't ever give up, no matter how long the course

My dreams are my lifeline, and I must follow them to the source.

Gratifying Soul

I.

I am proud to be a human being,

A part of the world, my home,

My family, friends and peers,

My identity, my very own.

II.

 I am proud to be alive,

And to be part of something greater,

Where I can learn and thrive,

Living for more than myself, that's what matters.

III.

 I am proud to be a girl,

In a world of diversity and light,

Where I can follow my dreams,

No matter what, I will make it right.

IV.

 I am proud to be a part,

Of this world of learning and surprises,

Where I can make a difference,

And be seen through my own eyes.

V.

 I am proud to be a human,

In a world of possibilities and change,

Where I can be the voice,

Of the silent and unseen, I will not be strange.

VI.

 I am proud to be me,

In a world of love and respect,

Where I can share my story,

And make a difference, no one can neglect.

VII.

 I am proud to be alive,

In this world of joy and sorrow,

Where I can fight injustice,

And make my voice heard, I will not cower.

VIII.

 I am proud to be a human,

In this world of challenges and hope,

Where I can take a stand,

And make a change, no matter how small, I will cope.

IX.

I am proud to be a girl,

Living in a world of possibilities and dreams,

Where I can share my voice,

And make a difference, I am not what it seems.

X.

 I am proud to be alive,

In this world of beauty and grace,

Where I can be me,

And not be afraid, I will own my space.

Heart's Wish

I.
Live your life as your heart directs,
Listen to what it suggests,
It will keep you on the right track,
And it won't ever lead you astray.

II.
 Find the courage to break free,
From the chains of society,
Follow your heart and make it known,
Live your life and make your own.

III.
 Don't be afraid of the unknown,
Your heart will guide you to your goal,
Take the risks and make a stand,
Live your life and make a plan.

IV.
 Take the time to be yourself,
Fulfill your dreams and explore your health,
Dare to be different and unique,
Live your life and be complete.

V.

Do not follow the crowd,
Follow what your heart allows,
It will lead you to the light,
And you will be free of fright.

VI.

Don't let your heart be broken,
Follow your dreams and don't be token,
Live an honest and true life,
Be happy and find the light.

VII.

Feel the joy that comes from within,
Follow your intuition and never give in,
Live your life as your heart directs,
Be happy, you'll never regret.

VIII.

Find the courage to take chances,
Go beyond the limits of advances,
Living life as your heart directs,
Will make you a masterpiece.

IX.

Don't be afraid to make mistakes,
Learn from them and never break,

Live your life and never be fake,

Be true to yourself and never break.

X.

 Remember to never give up,

Regardless of what life throws up,

Your heart will guide you and make you strong,

Live your life and enjoy it all along.

Adroit Zest

I.

I understand myself, in a girl's perspective,

As I walk through life, I must choose my path.

Sometimes I stumble, sometimes I fall,

But I must find a way to stand tall.

I have my own ambitions and dreams,

My own ideas and schemes,

And I know that I must strive,

To make them come alive.

I have my own beauty and grace,

My own power and place,

And I must not be afraid,

To show my true self to the world.

I must remember that I am strong,

No matter what I do, I can't be wrong,

And I must believe in myself and my worth,

And be confident in my own identity.

I must take courage and take each step,

No matter how far I have to go,

My path will be unique and my own,

And I must choose what's best for me.

II.

I understand myself, in a girl's perspective,

That I am capable of anything I choose to do.

I have the power to make my dreams come true,

And I must never give up no matter what I go through.

I must learn to be independent and brave,

And never let anyone make me feel enslaved.

I must find strength within me and never be afraid,

To face the world and make my own way.

I must never forget the power of my voice,

And speak out for what I believe is right.

I must be open to new ideas and opportunities,

And seize the chance to make a change.

I must be brave and follow my heart,

Believe in myself, no matter how far apart.

I must be kind, generous and loving,

And accept who I am, even when things aren't going.

Relishing Warm

I.

A feeling of soul satisfaction,

That I can't find in any other place,

A comfort that I can't replace,

It eclipses the hurt and pain of my past.

II.

From within I feel a spark,

My spirit ignited with joy,

A happiness that can't be destroyed,

My soul contentment I can't deny.

III.

A feeling of pure contentment,

A bliss that I can't explain,

A joy that no one can take away,

My soul satisfaction is here to stay.

IV.

I have found fulfillment within myself,

A sense of peace and contentment,

A joy that I can't deny,

My soul satisfaction shines bright.

V.

I have found satisfaction in my heart,

A joy that brings smiles to my face,

A feeling that can't be replaced,

My soul contentment is my saving grace.

VI.

A feeling of soul satisfaction,

A peace that can't be disturbed,

A joy that can't be measured,

My soul contentment brings me pleasure.

VII.

I have found contentment deep within,

A feeling that I can't ignore,

A bliss that is hard to find,

My soul satisfaction I can't deny.

VIII.

A feeling of pure bliss,

A contentment that can't be explained,

A joy that I can't replace,

My soul satisfaction is here to stay.

IX.

I have found joy within my heart,

A feeling that I can't ignore,

A bliss that can't be measured,

My soul satisfaction brings me pleasure.

X.

A feeling of pure bliss,

A joy that can't be explained,

A contentment that I can't deny,

My soul satisfaction is here to stay.

About the Author

Theva Kiruba

Theva Kiruba is an Indian Poetess, Podcaster and an Aspiring individual with high creative Intelligence who carving for her in depth thought to splash the sparkling colors to the World. Young published author. She holds Bachelor degree in English, Bachelors in education and pursuing her Master's in Holy Cross College, Trichy, India. She is really dynamic about spending her time in writing. She has developed strong sense of writing poetry. She has published more than 100 poems in various anthologies, as well as the books titled "A Quill with Nectar Drop", "Half Human", "The Girl's Secrete Wardrobe". She has received "InkQuill holder award" and "The Noble award" for her excellence in writing field.